Leaves ar

ANDREW FUSEK PETERS
Leaves are Like Traffic Lights

ANDREW FUSEK PETERS has written and edited over 80 books for young people, many with his wife Polly Peters. His books have won an American Library Association Notable Award, made the IBBY Honor list, been nominated for the Carnegie (twice), chosen as Sunday Times Children's Book Of The Week (twice) and featured as Guardian Children's Book Of The Week (three times). His author performances worldwide are renowned for their dynamic liveliness and infectious enthusiasm. His poems have appeared on Poetry Please, Radio 3 Words & Music, Blue Peter and CBeebies Poetry Pie. He also features on the Poetry Archive, with different material for both primary and secondary age ranges.

His poetry collections include *Mad, Bad & Dangerously Haddock* (Lion) "a very good overview of the kind of thing Fusek Peters does best and will please his multitudes of fans." Adele Geras, *Armadillo*. Andrew's anthology *Here's a Little Poem* (Walker/Candlewick) co-edited with Jane Yolen, was a Booklist Editor's Choice of the best books of the year and Sunday Times Children's Book of the Week. "A treat of an anthology" *Observer*. "Wonderful" *Independent*. "Fabulous." *Daily Telegraph*. His poems have also appeared in over 100 anthologies, including the *Oxford Book of Children's Poetry*.

For older readers, with Polly Peters, he wrote the Carnegie-nominated *Poems With Attitude* "It is rare and welcome to find a collection that speaks so directly to teenagers" *The Guardian*.

His novels include *Ravenwood* (Chickenhouse), published worldwide, 'Andrew has created a world to match the best classic fantasy series — breathtaking in its imaginative detail, almost Shakespearean in its telling,' Barry Cunningham.

Andrew lives in Shropshire with his wife and two children, and is addicted to playing squash and wild swimming at all times of the year.

Also by Andrew Fusek Peters

FOR CHILDREN:
Ravenwood (Chickenhouse/BBC Audio Books/Scholastic USA, 14 countries 2011)
Switching On The Moon, co-editor Jane Yolen (Walker/Candlewick, 2010)
The No-No Bird, co-author Polly Peters (Frances Lincoln, 2008)
Falcon's Fury, co-author Polly Peters (Frances Lincoln, 2008)
Skateboard Detectives Priceless & Diamonds Are For Evil (Orchard, 2008)
Mad, Bad and Dangerously Haddock: The Best of Andrew Fusek Peters (Lion, 2006)
Spies Unlimited (OUP, 2006)
Ghosts Unlimited (OUP, 2006)
Roar! Bull! Roar!, co-author Polly Peters (Frances Lincoln, 2006)
Here's A Little Poem, co-editor Jane Yolen (Walker/Candlewick, 2006)
Crash, co-author Polly Peters (Hodder 2005/DBDA, 2010)
Hubble Bubble: A Potent Brew of Magical Poems, editor (Hodder-Wayland, 2003)
Sheep Don't Go To School, editor (Bloodaxe, 1996)

FOR YOUNG ADULT:
Out Of Order: On the Edge Poems, editor (Evans, 2001/2009)
Poems With Attitude, co-author Polly Peters (Hodder-Wayland, 2001, Wayland, 2008)
Plays With Attitude, four titles, co-author Polly Peters (Evans, 2007/8)

ANDREW FUSEK PETERS

Leaves are Like Traffic Lights

Children's Poetry Library
No. 12

SALT

London

PUBLISHED BY SALT PUBLISHING
Dutch House, 307-308 High Holborn,
London WC1V 7LL United Kingdom

All rights reserved

© Andrew Fusek Peters, 2011
Illustrations © Asa Peters, 2011
Cover illustration © Chris Knight, 2011

The right of Andrew Fusek Peters to be identified as the
editor of this work has been asserted by him in accordance
with Section 77 of the Copyright, Designs and Patents Act 1988.

This book is in copyright. Subject to statutory exception
and to provisions of relevant collective licensing
agreements, no reproduction of any part may take
place without the written permission of Salt Publishing.

First published 2011

Printed in the UK by Lightning Source UK Ltd

Typeset in Oneleigh 11 / 14

*This book is sold subject to the conditions that it shall not,
by way of trade or otherwise, be lent, re-sold, hired out,
or otherwise circulated without the publisher's prior consent
in any form of binding or cover other than that in which
it is published and without a similar condition including this
condition being imposed on the subsequent purchaser.*

ISBN 978 1 84471 277 9 paperback

1 3 5 7 9 8 6 4 2

To my son Asa, the budding artist

CONTENTS

Acknowledgements	xi
Leaves are Like Traffic Lights	1
Fight to the Death	2
Trees Don't Go to School	3
The Time-Travelling Leaf	6
Autumn Rhythms	7
Top Secret Weather Report [Decoded]	8
Guy *Forks*	10
Leaf Song	11
My Brother the Tree	12
The No-No Bird	13
Hare Piece	14
The City Breathing	16
Easy Beyond Be*leaf*	18
December	19
Winter Garden Birds	20
Sledge	24
Winter Cookbook	26
Oak	27
Winter	28
Too Late Results	29
Imagination	30
Thief	32
The Gold-Leaf Gangster	34

What a Lark!	36
A Fussy Riddle	37
Keep Out!	38
Arrest That Tree!	39
Rhythm of the Day	42
The Rubbish Man	44
Riddle-Me-Read	46
The Magician	47
The Hills are Alive With the Sound of Knitting	48
I Know That You Might Think It Odd	50
Journey of a Tree	52
Water-Cycle	54
Alder	55
The Last Tree in the World	56
The Safest Place in the World	58
Pigeon	60
No Skateboarding Allowed	61
Ballad of the Trees	62
Rain Song	64
Dambusters	65
The Old Mansion	66
Forest Fire, Greece	68
Loop the Loop	70
Summer Swim	71
Sunset	72

Tide & Seek	73
Night & Day	74
Riddle Me Time	75
Forest School	76
Forestry Commission Meeting Minutes	78
Slash & Burn	80
1. Lift That Leg, Doggy!	81
2. The Tree's Reply	82
A Very Thin Riddle	84
A Tidy Poem	85
Sellout	86
Superfast	88
The Whole Wide Wood	90
Chant	92
Answers To Riddles	93

ACKNOWLEDGEMENTS

Poems in this collection were first published in the following publications:

'Top Secret Weather Report' in *Spies Unlimited* (OUP, 2006); 'Night & Day' in *The Upside Down Frown* (Hodder, 1998); 'Rhythm Of The Day', 'The Old Mansion', 'The Gold-Leaf Gangster', 'The Hills Are Alive With The Sound Of Knitting', 'The Safest Place In The World', 'Ballad Of The Trees', 'A Tidy Poem' and 'Leaf Song', in *The Moon Is On The Microphone* (Sherbourne, 2000); 'Summer Swim' first published as 'The Pool' in *101 Favourite Poems*, (Collins, 2002); 'Tide & Seek' and 'The No-No Bird' in *Here's A Little Poem*, (Walker, 2006); 'Guy Forks' in *Sling A Jammy Doughnut* (Hodder-Wayland, 2001); 'Winter', 'Riddle Me Tree' and 'A Fussy Riddle' in *Sheep Don't Go To School*, (Bloodaxe, 1996); 'Rain Song' in *Switching On The Moon* (Walker, 2010); 'My Brother The Tree' in *Mad, Bad & Dangerously Haddock, the best of Andrew Fusek Peters* (Lion, 2006); 'Forestry Commission Meeting Minutes' in *The Weather's Getting Verse* (Sherbourne, 1996); 'Water Cycle' in *Poems About Water* (Evans, 2007); 'The Time Travelling Leaf' in *Poems About Earth* (Evans, 2007); 'Chant' in *Sadderday & Funday* (Hodder, 2001).

'Leaves Are Like Traffic Lights' and 'Last Night I Saw The City Breathing' were broadcast on *Wham Bam Strawberry Jam*, (BBC1, 1996). 'The Magician' amd 'Rhythm of the Day' were broadcast on *Talking Poetry* (Radio 4, 1995). 'Trees Don't Go To School' was broadcast on *Blue Peter* (BBC1, 1992).

'Forest School' was written by Andrew Fusek Peters and Polly Peters. 'The Whole Wide Wood' was written by Polly Peters.

Leaves are Like Traffic Lights

LEAVES ARE LIKE TRAFFIC LIGHTS

Leaves are like traffic lights
on the trunk-road
of slow-moving seasons.
They go
Green,
Yellow,
Red.
The Summer stops!
The sun is switched off!
The trees become
a multi-coloured traffic jam!

Then,
a crazy wind drives straight through the forest tall,
makes each and every leaf
fall and crash
into the pile-up of Autumn,

and we
hoot and holler,
dive and dash,
scream and dream
and jump in the mess of shining, twisted leaves.
This happy accident of once a year
where no-one is hurt, and nobody grieves.

ANDREW FUSEK PETERS

FIGHT TO THE DEATH

Throw a stick into a tree
To catch a falling mystery.
Meteors now hit the ground
With a velvet, thumping sound.
Peel their green and pithy skin,
Soak in vinegar, find a tin.
Bake them like a loaf of bread,
Drill a hole right through each head.
Tie them with a length of string,
With a swoop, they're orbiting
Around your fingers, tightly curled
They zoom, two stones that have been hurled.
Like asteroids, they crash mid-flight;
Oh nothing beats a conker fight!
How to find the winner? It's
Whose conker ends up not in bits!

Leaves are Like Traffic Lights

TREES DON'T GO TO SCHOOL

Trees don't go to school,
won't sit still and muck about lots.
Trees are messy, never comb their hair
and once a year
they dare to cover our clean concrete streets
with their dirty brown leaves!
Trees definitely deserve detentions!

Trees keep on growing,
NO matter how much you shout at them
but in the end, just like you
they can be hurt.

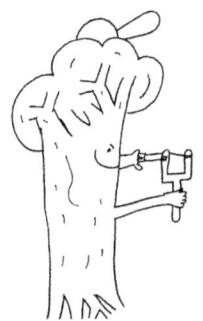

3

'Daydreaming again little Larch?
When the boss hears of this
he'll chop you into little bits!
Out with the chainsaw
and little Larchy is no more!
In ten days time you'll be shiny and neat,
finishing your life as a wooden toilet seat!'

Hang on a second ...
Trees have had enough!
We will not be sat on anymore!
Trees on truant!

We want to wake with the soft dawn,
let the sun melt us into day,
hear the birds sing inside us!

Trees on truant!
If you keep cutting us down,
we'll hold our breath
until the world turns blue
and no-one can breathe.

WE INTERRUPT THIS POEM FOR AN EMERGENCY NEWSFLASH!

'Yesterday it was reported that a young beech tree
was caught streaking stark naked
through the quiet streets of Winter.
One blind resident complained,
"Ugh! All those rude branches dancing nude in the wind,
with not even a leaf to cover herself!
It's disgusting and shouldn't be allowed!"
The government has reacted by issuing a standard set
of white cotton underpants to every tree in the country.'

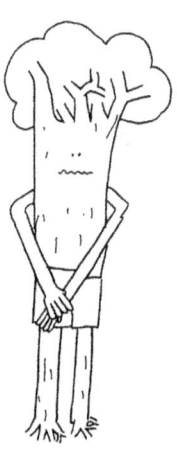

ANDREW FUSEK PETERS

THE TIME-TRAVELLING LEAF

I
Now sigh
And fly down
From tree top crown,
Fall and flutter, sleep,
Compost, compressed, lie deep.
Years in millions are my goal,
This dream becomes a seam of *coal*.
More time crawls by, will not be rushed
Watch as my black heart is crushed!
Transformed, my carbon weight
Meets its fiery fate.
Diamonds are sharp
Sings my harp.
This rare
Flare

AUTUMN RHYTHMS

Cold Rivers
Cat's Shivers
Leaf Skivers
Sky Divers
Air Shak-Attack-A-Make-Me-Quake
Sun Drinking Sky
Night Thinking Sigh
It's Over
Gone Clover
No Flowers
Now Showers
Blues
Flu's
Autumn
Caught 'em.

TOP SECRET WEATHER REPORT [DECODED]

Today,
the sky was undercover
and the weather was definitely up to no good.
Raindrops tapped out their secret codes on rooftops
and finally managed to infiltrate puddles.

Today,
the sun was in disguise.
No-one would recognise her
in those nondescript baggy clothes.
Our organisation on the ground
began to doubt
if she ever even existed.

Today,
the clouds were on guard duty,
walkie-talkies blaring thunder
with wheeling crows for sunglasses

Today,
Autumn was betrayed
and the trees were shaking with fear.
The ground was sprinkled with leaf-codes
and the wind riffled through the endless golden piles
trying to work out what they meant.

Today,
bonfires sent out secret smoke signals,
roasted chestnuts were too hot to handle
and soon, if all went according to plan,
there would be
FIREWORKS!

ANDREW FUSEK PETERS

GUY FORKS

The hill above London Town
Is filled with a feast of light,
Catherine Wheels are Custard Creams
Spinning like sweets in the night.

Sparklers dance their sherbert fizz,
Blown out by the wind so sour,
Rockets leap like liquorice lace,
And explode in a sugar shower.

Bangers go plop in a mushy mash,
The flames are eating the Guy.
Chestnuts tap-dance on the coals,
And *taste like heaven!* I sigh.

Hot dogs warm as the bonfire,
With mustard sharp as the cold,
November the fifth is a feast,
For this hungry seven year old!

LEAF SONG

Said the leaf to the sky,
I would learn how to fly,
But I'm shaking like a leaf, do I dare?

Said the sky to the leaf,
It's a matter of belief,
Just jump into my blanket of air!

Then the sky sang,
Then the leaf sprang,
And the trees were empty and bare.

ANDREW FUSEK PETERS

MY BROTHER THE TREE

My brother, a tree so strong, and I
Remember climbing way up high.

My brother, bent over, suddenly sick,
Thin as a twig, snapped like a stick.

My brother, a bonfire built in the dark,
Spitting out one final spark.

My brother, by morning, a cold, grey heap
Curled up in the ash, is this how you sleep?

My brother, a jostle of leaves in my head
Whispering all of the words you said.

My brother, an acorn, a listening ear,
A cup to pour out every fear.

Through all the years you shelter me:
My brother the once and always tree.

THE NO-NO BIRD

I'm the no-no bird
That's right, that's me.
I live up in
The Tantrum Tree.

I'm the no-no bird,
I won't say why
I stamp my feet
And shout and cry.

I'm the no-no bird!
I sulk and sing
No! No! No!
To everything.

ANDREW FUSEK PETERS

HARE PIECE

Crows are conjuring the dusk.
The moon's a bitten bit of rusk.

Buzzard sings her mewing cry,
Prowling, feathered cat-of-sky

And there among the winter beet
I'm given grace, a priceless treat

For tired, telescopic eyes:
Two hares, and then to my surprise

They stand, each balanced like a boy
Their stance a circus trick of joy.

They push out paws, begin to fight,
A furry flash of grey and white,

Such a bold and brave display
As on hind legs they swerve and sway,

Ears stuck up like lollipops,
I breathe too loud, the battle stops.

Leaves are Like Traffic Lights

They turn to statues cut from bark.
I blink. They sprint into the dark,

Leaving me to simply stare
At a dream no longer there.

Oh what delights this world unlocks
To let me see two hares that box.

THE CITY BREATHING

Last night, I saw the City breathing
great gusts of people,
rushing in and
puffing out
of stations' singing mouths.

Last night, I saw the City laughing.
Takeaways got the giggles,
cinemas split their sides
and living rooms completely creased themselves!

Last night, I saw the City dancing.
Shadows were cheek to cheek with brick walls,
trains wiggled their hips all over the place
and the trees
in the breeze,
put on a show for an audience of windows!

Last night, I saw the city starving.
Snaking Avenue smacked her lips
and swallowed seven roundabouts!
Fat office blocks got stuffed with light
and gloated over empty parking lots.

Last night, I saw the City crying.
Cracked windows poured falling stars
and the streets were paved with mirrors.

Last night, I saw the City sleeping.
Roads night-dreamed,
street lamps quietly boasted,
"When I grow up, I'm going to be a star!"
and the wind,
like a cat,
snoozed in the nooks of roofs.

ANDREW FUSEK PETERS

EASY BEYOND BEL*EAF*

A Riddle

Some say that I am barking,
I've finally gone to the dogs!
(In fact it's the other way round!)
This is easy as falling off logs.

In Winter I go starkers,
In summer I get dressed.
Listen Bud, it's simple!
Have you twigged yet? Have you guessed?

DECEMBER

At dusk, the smudgy trees
Have fallen to their knees,
Praying to the night
To keep them safe from sight.

The rooks rise up in flocks
Like dark, electric shocks.
They settle, silence falls,
And something in me calls.

The fields are charged and changed
Their shapes are dim, deranged,
Strange echoes of the day
Now softening to grey.

The distant houses lit
Like beacons far off shore
And I a drifting boat,
Shall reach my home once more, once more
Shall reach my home once more.

WINTER GARDEN BIRDS

BLACKBIRD

Fat as blackberry pie.
How do you still take off?
Bright orange bladed beak
stabs for seeds.

WREN

A bumbling brown ball of small
hops in the hollow of hedge.
Mini magician,
"Now you see me! Now you . . ."

NUTHATCH

Ballet-bat of the bird world,
upside down hanger-on,
glued to the feeder.
Nutaholic!

BLUE TITS

Timid twittering gangs,
kitted out in yellow and blue.
Ready to flee
at the smallest smidgen of sound.

ROBIN

Puffed-up, paint-splodged,
stage-struck strutter.
An orange light bulb in the leafless gloom.

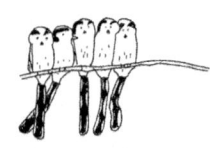

LONG-TAILED TITS

Black and white lollipops,
scribbled streaks that swoop in mobs,
by night, huddle in hidden hedge for warmth.

HOUSE SPARROWS

Suburbs' best mates.
Eave-delvers,
scrabbling-scratchers by night.
Unremarkable lawn hoppers,
Sadly rarer year by year.

SLEDGE

The cold is a shark, snapping at my face
and this slope is as steep as danger.
I step up and up like a sideways crab
dragging my sledge on a string.
At last, at the top,
Dad sinks down, squeezed at the back,
parks his boots like brakes.
"All aboard!" he shouts.
I snuggle into the cave of his arms,
suddenly scared.
"Grab the handles, hold on tight!"
A push and we're off!
The hill grabs us,
chucks us over the edge like a stone.
Down we bolt with a blur
skim through slush
as flakes fly into my eyes
and all of me roars with excitement.

We hit a hidden bump.
And there we are,
in the middle of the air!
For a second, I *get* what it's like to fly . . .

We crump back to earth
in a flurry of arms and legs,
tumble and spin like a washing machine
while the snow is a nosy cat,
curling round toes,
prowling down my neck.
"Again!" I scream, soaking, frozen and smiling.
And again and again
until the moon slides over the sky,
round and white as a dream.

WINTER COOKBOOK

Sprinkle a spoonful of stars
around topmost twigs,
then turn the temperature down
and allow bark to bake
slowly over night.
Brush with freezing breezes.
Wait.

In the morning,
take out the sun from the east,
spread beams thin like butter,
dab branches with icing sugar.
As dawn breaks through the clouds,
add a touch of twinkle.
To finish,
serve with frosted flakes
on a bed of snow.

Works each time, this recipe
as eyes now feast on every tree.

OAK

The oak is such a clever tree
With leaves that learn from history,
Waiting for the wind to call
Knowing just the time to fall
As Winter, with a bully's strength
Rides the wooded breadth and length.
But though he does his best to brawl,
The tree, now shorn, withstands it all,
Hunkered down into a dream
Where wind can do no more than scream.
Bare of leaves, it seems to me,
The oak is such a clever tree.

ANDREW FUSEK PETERS

WINTER

In the night,
Came a white horse to visit,
His hooves made no sound
As he covered the ground,
And snow filled the land with its spirit.

Traditional Czech

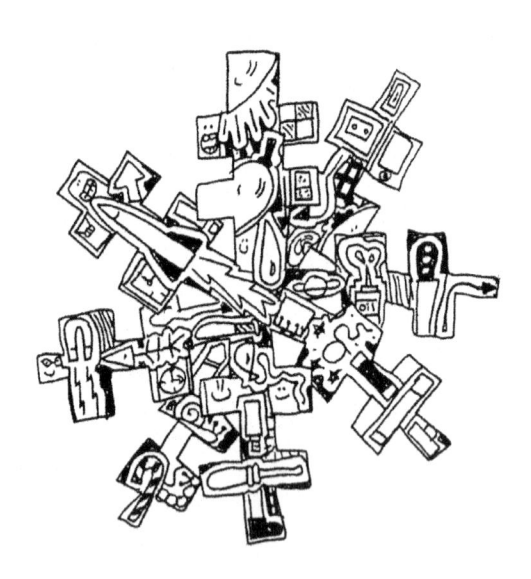

Leaves are Like Traffic Lights

TOO LATE RESULTS

Roving Motorways 1
Nature Wanderers 0

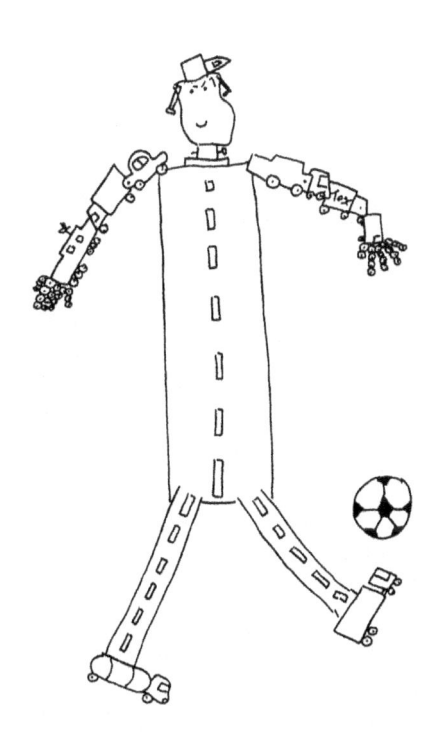

IMAGINATION

"New health and safety regulations require pupils visiting streams to wear wellington boots and rubber gloves in case they catch diseases."

A boy had a bag of dreams.
It was filled with
impossible ideas, annoying noises
and dangerous dares.

The boy went to school.
When it snowed outside,
he peeked in his bag.
There were:
snowballs and slides,
clouds made from breath and brilliant bruises.
The door to the playground stayed locked.

The boy went to school,
where a tree stood alone in a field.
He climbed inside his bag.
There were
handholds and hidden heights.
At the top, a whole class of views
was learning how to dream,
but the tree was out of bounds.

The boy went to school,
to do a project on rivers.
He dived into his bag.
There were splashes and screams,
a nice new net and oodles of wet.
Instead,
they studied the properties of water
and the real stream wept as it wound its way.

The boy was so angry,
he emptied his bag
and the rules blew away in a blizzard,
leaving only a lonely tree.
For a dare,
the boy leapt into the sky.
When the snow melted,
he dreamed up a river,
and a dangerous horse
that he rode all the way
with his bag of dreams
to the sea, the sea,
the impossible blue-black sea.

THIEF

A thief came by in the night
To pilfer our dreams and delight.

He drank rivers dry with a straw,
Shoved the woods to the back of a drawer,
Snatched up birds while on the wing,
Wrapped the fields with balls of string,
Squeezed the hills into a box,
Tied it tight with chains and locks,
Left the landscape bare and torn
Like a sheep now newly shorn.

He planted towers row on row,
Then smiled to watch them grow and grow,
Stretched the streets into spaghetti,
Sprinkled people like confetti;
Threw them down a bunch of shops,
Scattered cash like lollipops,
Filled the streets with cars that cough,
Made the trees, like cheese, go off,
Finished with a concrete floor:
Welcome to the land of More!
Then he switched his new gift on
And clapped to see how it all shone.
Wondrous beacon of the night:
City dreaming of delight.

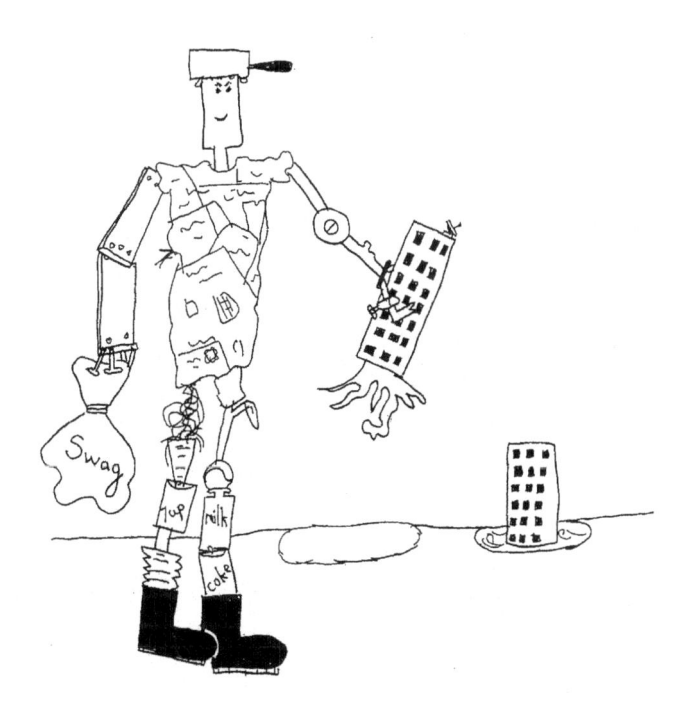

Leaves are Like Traffic Lights

THE GOLD-LEAF GANGSTER

Autumn:
Summer sighed,
sat down
and Winter offered her a cup of tea.

Autumn:
Summer's gone,
took her summer holiday.

Autumn:
friend of sly Winter,
the Gold-Leaf Gangster.
This man is wanted for doing the strip-trees
and stealing summer's colour photos.
For the next three months,
it's only black and white.

Autumn:
Summer's so sad
she went for a night out on the town
and afterwards,
couldn't remember a thing.

Hot and bothered Nature
bought an air freshener.
But cool Winter got a bit too fresh,
made his big mistake
when he kissed the sleeping beauty,
Spring!

WHAT A LARK!

Well, there's a lot of birds and things
makin' a hell of a racket
and, like, flowers stickin' out of the the ground,
everyone's sellin' 'em, makin' a packet,
bit of colour,
know what I mean?

So, right, saw the sun
hangin' out down the street,
had a bit of a chat,
me and her, you know, "how's the weather?"
Stuff like that.

The lambs have gone bananas, bonkers!
Right off their rockers they are!
I dunno really,
this Spring thing,
it's just happenin',
so there you go, eh!
Bish! Bash! Bosh!
La-di-da!

Leaves are Like Traffic Lights

A FUSSY RIDDLE

One day, it swept in through the door,
rushed and fussed around the floor
then jumped inside our wooden chest!
What can it be? Just one clue more:
it grew up in a forest . . .

Traditional Czech

KEEP OUT!

Evil-natured nature
sprang Spring
by smuggling in
a paintbrush
and a bit of blush.

To the inmates' surprise,
before their eyes,
there burst a riot of colour:
Wood Anemones,
golden Celandine
and velvet Bluebell
all deserved a good spell behind bars!

Soon, they were back in the nick,
spools of barbed wire did the trick.
A 'PRIVATE!' sign,
'This land is mine!'
and everything's fine
once again.

ARREST THAT TREE!

There were rumours that ran round the woods
That Tree-face had gone underground.
Though even if true, we agreed,
No excuses, the Tree will be found!

Though he'd shaved off all of his leaves
And was wearing a snow-white disguise,
We found out where he was hiding, said,
"Hey Bud! No more of your lies!"

Mister Tree was playing it cool,
He was shifty and smooth as ice,
"Just tell us the truth, you old trunk,
Or I promise we won't play nice!"

We took out the sun and trained it,
But Mister Tree said not a thing.
With a mouth that was quiet as twilight,
Like a black-bird, we hoped he would sing.

At last we grew close to the truth
And his lies began melting away.
With a drip, drip we wore him right down
All through the lengthening day.

But suddenly! He pulled such a fast one.
You should have seen him spring!
We ducked as the buds went flying
And here's the curious thing:

One second — he was well in our sight,
The next, quite beyond belief,
He unfurled a camouflage coat
And was gone in the green of a leaf.

Leaves are Like Traffic Lights

RHYTHM OF THE DAY

and the rain and the rain on the window pane
alarm and awake and "I'm hungry Mum!"
and the rain and the post and soldiers on toast
with tea.

and me and my brother
and the chatter and the clatter
and the buzz on the bus on the way to school
and smiles and crisps and bags on backs
with books.

and socks in shoes are wet as the sea
and the friends and the class so brightly lit
and we dream and it steams the windows up
and it's safe.

and the rain and the rain and the rain is beating
sleeting, world-defeating
a cough and a shiver and stamping of feet
oh when will the storm be over?

and the rain is a pain that has gone away
and the clouds so proud are sulking
and the day is long and on and on

with sun and fun and hide and seek
'til mum calls out with a cry and a shout
oh why do we have to go home?

and we run and pour though lane and door
and the clatter and the chatter of knives and forks
and nice hot food and a big fat tum
and the sun has begun to set.

and a bath and a bath and a simmering bath
poking, joking, everyone's soaking
a race and a race, first place to bed
and the sky in the night is filled with stars
and the room is full of whispers
and a sleep and a sleep and it's time to sleep
and a sleep and a sleep and I'm counting sheep
and asleep and asleep and I'm falling deep.

ANDREW FUSEK PETERS

THE RUBBISH MAN

I'm the Rubbish Man,
Prince of Plastic, King of Tin Can.
People say I'm disgusting,
But the children are so trusting
When I rip (*or do they throw?*)
Such sweet wrappers from their hands
To scatter them brightly across the lands.

I am the Reveller of Rags,
Emperor of Empty Shopping Bags.

Yes! I'm the Rubbish Man!
Catch me, Collar me, Collect me if you can.
It's me who stole into your sleep,
Took your mattress soft and deep.
Now, I'm coiled up, comfortably rusting by the
      Rubbish Stream
As She slips her way through the city's dark dream.

Oh! I'm the Rubbish Man!
Rubbing out wishes as only I can.
I made the blocks that burn the sky
And if you dare to ask me why,
I'll say it's my job, it's what I do.
Then will I dance The Rubbish Dance for you.

For, I'm the Rubbish Man!
Bin me, Bag me, Beat me if you can,
But together we'll dance all days away
And Darkness, my friend, shall come to stay.

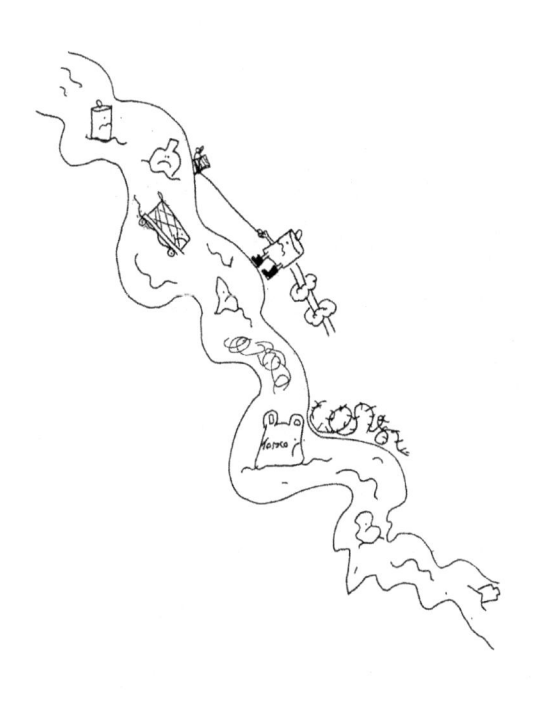

ANDREW FUSEK PETERS

RIDDLE-ME-READ

Thunder storer
Silent roarer
Life container
Fib sustainer
Boredom cracker
Yawn attacker
Happy ending
Good for lending
On the shelf
By myself
Full of words
that fly like birds
Never die
What am I?

THE MAGICIAN

Blue was the sky, blue as a blade,
made to cut the clouds from high,
floating feathers that fell to the sea,
white as a wave with a foaming sigh.

But the sun felt tired, decided to set,
set down her bed, unfolded her quilt
of strawberry-red. Curled like a flower
she fell into dream and day began to wilt.

Night strolled by, dressed in dark,
with a blanket of black, he blinded the sky,
clicked his fingers, struck a spark
and the sky was a pirate with a silver eye.

He took off his hat of infinite deep,
stars like rabbits shot from their sleep.
From his sleeves came a handkerchief, soft and grey,
with a flourish it shimmered as the Milky Way.

How the trees clapped for Magician Night!
How the sea cried one foaming tear!
Now the hills sing in his shadowy light.
Now the land waits for day to draw near.

THE HILLS ARE ALIVE WITH THE SOUND OF KNITTING

Last night, my Auntie Madge
knitted a couple of hills.
She got the pattern from a magazine,
KNITTING TODAY!
'For colourful effect, add animals, two or three, say.'
So she crocheted a bobble of bleating sheep
and into the hills they creep, they creep.
All night it took my Auntie Madge.

"How about some day?" she beamed,
and wove it ray by ray
till her fingers were so sore,
but Aunt Madge, she saw
that it was good.

'Next,' said the magazine, *'you could try
a few seam-stitches to cover the sky!'*
It seemed she needed her knitting machine,
took out her Singer, that sang so loud,
birds awoke, stitch turned to cloud.
Aunt Madge sat back, satisfied,
"I shall call it . . . Countryside!"

Then along came a man, striding, striding
wearing a pair of concrete shoes.
"Hear my news!" he said,
as he snagged the thread,
and under his tread
unravelled the land.

ANDREW FUSEK PETERS

I KNOW THAT YOU MIGHT THINK IT ODD

I know that you might think it odd
but I believe that the tree that waits
at the top of my lane
is a god.

Yes, I can truly sense your doubt:
This bunch of bark!
This messy mass is just a wodge of wood!
I simply ask that you would hear me out.

It's best to begin with geography:
this finely-fingered beech
sits astride a high-hilled copse,
a sentinel whose branches swing
like lullabies. A sanctuary

I clamber up,
into the leafy depths of June,
hidden in a green so deep
I would be drowned. And what a tune

is played within those boughs.
The scrape of wind is soft
as a rasping lick of cows.

Valleys open up their arms beneath;
the hills beyond, a splayed out
pack of cards,
wherein I hold the winning hand
that fills me with belief.

This is my childhood, chapel-of-ease,
my memories suspended here and high
above the earth, where I am buoyant
in the breeze.

So there you have my argument:
my secret priest that blesses fields
unfurling from her feet
and she still stands,
though years have bound and bent

her into a kind of grace that is no longer odd.
For I believe with all my heart
that the tree at the top of my lane
Is a god.

ANDREW FUSEK PETERS

JOURNEY OF A TREE

To be performed aloud

I'm standing around
in the wood, like you would
when along comes a guy with a chain saw,
that coughs like a crow with a caw.
Oh I'm swinging in the wind, then I sway,
fall with a crash, oh boy do I make their day!
I'm dragged through the muck, to the truck
in a hurry, on a lorry, to the mill,
where I spill my guts
get smashed and mashed
till I'm flat and thin as a sheet of tin.
Now Paper is my name
and blank is the game.

Along comes a human
with a hoard of words,
hidden down deep in the root-heart.
Art is a box that unlocks
and then
comes the scribble of the pen
as I'm filling up with dreams,
stuffed with schemes,
bound to delight
dressed to impress in black and white.

Leaves are Like Traffic Lights

Once a tree,
the story that you see,
is out there in the world,
like a bird flying free.
Take a look,
full of leaves once again,

I'm a book!

ANDREW FUSEK PETERS

WATER-CYCLE

Hot sun soak her up,
cold cloud spit her out,
with a shout of thunder
how she falls,
falls asleep, lies deep.
Mountains weep and dream
and in the dream she seems to grow,
stronger, longer,
full of river-longing
wide awake,
thrills like a milkshake shivers,
she spills into the land.
But then a man made hand
stops her dead with a dam.
Down, down, down underground,
rushing round,
pushed around by endless fists of metal
how she weeps.
Someone twists the tap.
Tap, kettle, cup of tea,
into me and out of me,
down the drain, underground,
rushing round
spilling into land
and filling out the sea
where the hot sun waits
how she sings!

ALDER

The old river bed is now dry
the stream has forsaken its course,
Its hooves have stamped a new valley
And its song is a galloping horse.

But how can the alder up sticks
As she rests by the old river bed
Where the wind makes a river of grass
And ripples with nettles instead?

For this tree made a bet on a river
That left her for pastures new
And the only drink to be had
Is a sip of the morning dew.

At night, she dreams of the stream
And the trout that broil in the burn.
Her heart is a murmur of leaves
That longs for the river's return.

THE LAST TREE IN THE WORLD

Yesterday it was reported that Mrs Beech had died.
She had no known relatives.
The only witness, a Mr C. Hainsaw said,
"I was so cut up about this,
old Beechy kept herself to herself,
sometimes she'd stand in the same place for years.
The police asked her to move on,
but she insisted her home was
in the middle of the pavement!
She was barking mad,
always going on about being the last of her kind."

When I'm gone, my boy,
the shock will take your breath away
I'm rare, I am! Now buzz off!

"I thought she was being rude about my medical condition,"
said Mr C. Hainsaw,
"It's not easy having rotating blades instead of arms,
nor was it my fault that I tripped over
and accidentally,
chopped her head off.
Poor Old Beechy ...
there was bud flying everywhere!
It was beyond be-leaf,
I called the *copse* straightaway

but they could see it was a genuine mistake!"
said Mr C. Hainsaw with obvious relief
as he sat on the stump of his throne,
totally innocent, totally alone.

THE SAFEST PLACE IN THE WORLD

Once I climbed
To the top of a tree.
Low lay the town,
Spread like a sea.

Branches bent
To make a seat,
The world swam by
Beneath my feet.

Roofs shone out,
Their blue-black tiles
Like scaly fish
With chimney smiles.

I had clambered
Out of a box,
A lid of leaves,
And me the fox . . .

No bullies to hunt me,
Where birds sing clear
I'm king of the wind!
I banish fear!

Leaves are Like Traffic Lights

The sun ran home
And stars fell out.
"Time for dinner!"
I heard Mum shout.

I slid down the slide
Built from bark,
Out of the sky
And into the dark.

PIGEON

The pigeon's such a flappy flier,
This clumsy lump does not inspire.
A feathered jelly dressed in grey
Common as a cloudy day;
And yet I would not be deterred
From praising this ungainly bird.
When day begins, her softly cry
Announces that the night's gone by.
So I for one am in her thrall
as branches echo with her call.

But be warned, you'll come to grief
If you stand right underneath.
Else she will do what she must do
And splatter you with pigeon poo!

NO SKATEBOARDING ALLOWED

My board is a bird, this pavement below me the sky.
Adults frown and tut, though I will never be deterred,
As I slalom with a smile for my alibi,
For my board is a bird.

I think these no-go rules are terribly absurd!
All I need is concrete and a rail where I can try
The latest tricks I have jealously seen and heard.

You see, I have this body that dreams that it can fly.
So grown-ups, don't be sour in giving us your word
To do your best to just this once imagine why,
My board is a bird.

ANDREW FUSEK PETERS

BALLAD OF THE TREES

In your words, I am an Oak tree.
I have been here a hundred years or more.
They tried to put me away in an old people's home,
but I'm still hanging about in the street like a tramp.
The earth is a good bed
and my blanket the wide sky.

Once,
I was round, small as your thumb
until my mother dropped me,
just like that.
I fell to the ground,
a dream inside a seed,
waiting.

Then,
this street was stripped of its bark
and underneath lay the muddy drover's path.
Horses ploughed your classroom and
wheat grew between your desks.
It is so easy to forget.

Leaves are Like Traffic Lights

Now,
in your words,
I am grown old.
The concrete hides me away,
and the street tries to run me over.
I wrap myself in bark
against this biting wind.

But if you stop
and listen,
I shall promise to sing you a song of leaves.
And if you dream,
dream the cold hearted cities away, away
dream the cold hearted cities away.

ANDREW FUSEK PETERS

RAIN SONG

Rockabye raindrops
Fall from the sky;
They tap-dance on tiles
A wild lullaby.

They gush through the gutters.
On smooth windowpanes,
They scribble and scrabble,
Then gargle down drains

To spatter and scatter
In silvery streams
With a cradle of wind
And rockabye dreams.

DAMBUSTERS

Find a river, build a dam
Into a stony snake.
Watch the water wriggle round
And leave behind a lake.

ANDREW FUSEK PETERS

THE OLD MANSION

The house stands still like a solitary crane
In a pool of deep green grass.
The windows dark as thundered rain,
Rooms all drowned in glass.

Shadow hen, now come to roost,
It pecked and gobbled the light.
Here, the house is only host
To the visiting fox of night.

House that once held charm and chime,
Now a bricked up box of air.
The thief has come and stolen time,
Silence dies: there's no-one there.

This house is a washed up lonely shell
On the grey and windswept lea.
But cup your ear and listen well
To the hiss of the far off sea.

Leaves are Like Traffic Lights

ANDREW FUSEK PETERS

FOREST FIRE, GREECE

Asleep on the beach
in the gritty sand of dreams
I woke to the foggy sense of smoke.
And there,
like a ragged trouser hem,
a line of fire unravelled down the hills.
I was glad of the sea behind me
but in front was a burning horizon;
more than a mile away,
yet the heat hit my face like a tan
and the crackling of trees filled my ears.

It was huge,
a lumbering, glowing snail,
unstoppable by any engine of man.
We rolled our towels,
retreated into town.
The square was empty, except for dust.
Behind wooden shutters
the people prayed for wind to intervene.

Leaves are Like Traffic Lights

That day, the breeze was kind
and every building sighed in relief
as I wondered
what mere spark, dropped cigarette
or worse,
malevolent match
had woken this roaring river of flame?

ANDREW FUSEK PETERS

LOOP THE LOOP

A Riddle

Shot like stones, flung from a sling,
Wheeling wildly wing to wing.
Zinging round the blue zip wire,
Fantastic feathered fury-flier.
Gossips on the telephone line,
Squawking under hot sunshine.
Sign of summer, have you guessed?
These loopy loopers are the best.

SUMMER SWIM

We wade through corn like tigers on fire
And run the obstacle course of barbed wire
To follow the stream in a winding dream
Until in a corner, scooped like ice cream,
Under the alders, a hidden pool;
I trail my fingers in the willowy cool.
The grass is bullied and nettles beaten,
Blankets laid for food to be eaten.
We leap like salmon one, two, three,
Divebombers of this inland sea,
Hit the water, bodies froze,
Suddenly trout are tickling toes.
The oak is a mast in the ship of shade,
Cows drift through the grassy glade,
Heads bent like old men reading the news,
As beyond, the hills hold distant views.
Under the beaming fat lady sun,
Witch of warmth, conjuring fun,
Until she grows tired and a little bit low
And daylight packs up, ready to go!
Oh why can't summer last forever,
And why can't we take home this river?
In twilight we stumble through itchy corn,
Get caught on barbed wire with trousers torn,
Sleepily falling into cars
To carry us home under rippling stars.

SUNSET

The sky's an orange layer cake,
Ready for the night to bake;
Stuffed with yellow, cloudy cream
And one last shiny sugar-beam.

The cowboy whipped out his lasso
To snare the feast before it flew.
He caught the sun and rode it hard,
All around the evening yard.

As day strode off into the west,
We all agreed this boy was best:
His mouth now filled with Cherry Jam,
Tip your hat to Sunset Sam!

Leaves are Like Traffic Lights

TIDE & SEEK

At night, the stars fall out of bed,
For them the dark is day instead.
The moon is bright, it's time to play,
Hide and seek with the Milky Way.

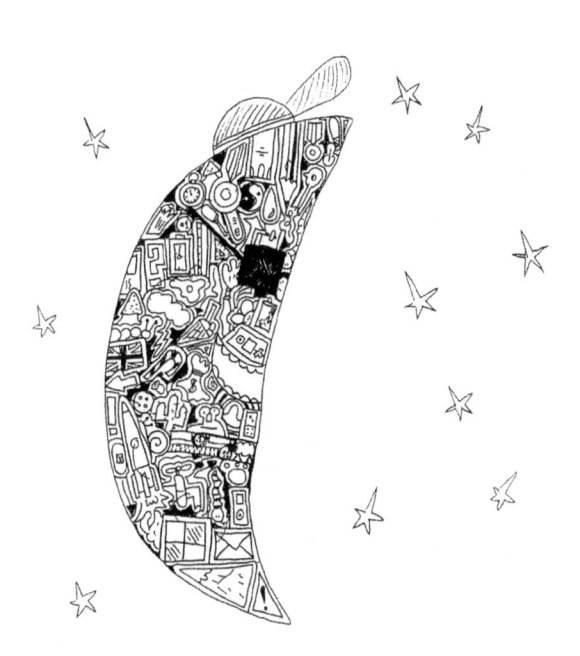

NIGHT & DAY

Onion Moon
In a bowl of night;
Sliver of silver,
Garnish of light.

Onion Sun
Peels night away;
Flaming tears
Deliver day.

Leaves are Like Traffic Lights

RIDDLE ME TIME

There stands an oak
and from that oak,
twelve branches grew,
and on each branch,
nests two plus two
and in each nest,
seven eggs bright blue.

Traditional Czech

FOREST SCHOOL

Gather twigs, lay a fire,
watch flames grow like saplings,
soar like skylarks.

Rain rattles down.
Only a shower,
quick! Dive into the den.
We shiver and scuff the dry-leaf floor, until
sun, like a biscuit crumbles down.

Everyone out! Wellies gloop and slurp
through the new, muddy puddles (we call
them 'muddles').
It's time for a mission!
Stick-hunting, branch-prowling,
sniffing out ten different shapes of leaf.
We are explorers, treasure-hunters
poking in hollows of towering trunks,
discoverers of smooth acorns, soft feathers,
sharp lumps of stone and bark in the shape of a bird.

Mrs Miller calls, 'One, two three,
where are you?'
It's time for snacks. We gather, on logs
with whittled sticks in fists.
One by one each name is called
and we're allowed
to spear marshmallows, reach carefully towards the
    embers' glow
and hear them sigh and hiss at the heat.
Then, with a curl and a crisping to brown, they're done:
squidged between biscuits, sweet sandwich of goo.

We gather all our bits and bobs
and later, at home time we rush out shouting,
'Look! We're taking home the forest
in a paper bag!'

Just imagine if, at teatime we shook out the whole wood
and poured out jugs of sky
and invited the trees to tea.

FORESTRY COMMISSION MEETING MINUTES

It was decided on this day,
by the Venerable Alder Councillors
that a new forest was to be built.

Sadly, this meant that much of the town
would be chopped down.
The people-mentalists were in uproar
"Not In My Back Yard!" they screamed,
and the trees just dreamed.

To make matters worse,
the hours, years and minutes
of the River Planning Sub-Commission
were found to have given permission
to run a river right through
the new Housing Estate.

"Soon, there'll be streams all over the place,
changing forever the face
of our tidy tarmac land!" they screamed,
and the trees just dreamed.

Leaves are Like Traffic Lights

The FPCC members,
(an August Branch of World Interest Incorporated)
listened to their words
flying like leaves in the winds of opinion . . .
and saved the worst until last.

People would also have to be cleared,
or it was feared that good trees might lose their jobs.
But in appreciation of the people-mentalists' point
    of view,
it was agreed that all bodies would be recycled —
leg cabins; fine finger bowls, unsoled foot-stools;
complete head cases.
And it is our intention to give a helping hand
to the arm-chair industry.

And so the trees that day, justly dreamed
and so the trees that day-dreamed, just dreamed.

SLASH & BURN

This is the burger that tastes so nice.

This is the burger that tastes so nice
That came from the cow that paid the price.

This is the burger that tastes so nice
That came from the cow that paid the price
That lived in a place that once was a wood.

This is the burger that tastes so nice
That came from the cow that paid the price
That lived in a place that once was a wood
That was chopped down and burned for good.

This is the burger that tastes so nice
That came from the cow that paid the price
That lived in a place that once was a wood
That was chopped down and burned for good
That once was a forest of wonder wild.

This is the burger that tastes so nice
That came from the cow that paid the price
That lived in a place that once was a wood
That was chopped down and burned for good
That once was a forest of wonder wild
That's now by man and fire defiled.

1. LIFT THAT LEG, DOGGY!

Little doggy visits tree,
Lifts his leg and has a wee.
So, went and bought a battery,
And wire to wrap accordingly.

Oh I found it hard to hide
The happiness I felt inside
The next time that the doggy tried,
And ended up — electrified.

2. THE TREE'S REPLY

Hang on! said the wise old tree,
It's a mystery to me

Why you blame the little dog
Who left behind a stinky log!

Follow up the leather lead
To find the answer that you need:

It's the owner who's a twit,
Who doesn't even care a bit,

Never, ever seems to mind
What her doggy's left behind.

If you'd like some justice done,
And revenge that's kind of fun,

Grab a leaf (you must be swift),
And roll that 'log' into a gift.

Then creep up like a thief with swag
And stuff it in her shoulder bag!

Now retreat, you've done enough
As it squishes round her stuff:

Smearing pen and mobile too,
It covers everything with goo!

When she gets home, just watch her eyes
As fingers find that small surprise!

That's justice! said the wise old tree,
For you've returned her property . . .

The owner of the dog, it's true
Is reunited with its poo!

ANDREW FUSEK PETERS

A VERY THIN RIDDLE

My heart's a flutter, my spirit's torn
When I think of the tree where I was born.
The sad, four-cornered truth is that,
Even now I feel so flat.
I am in shreds, so incomplete,
In death I've stayed as white as a sheet.
Was I buried? No it was a sin
That I was crumpled and chucked in the bin.
Can you guess why I'm covered in creases?
Pray for me, I'm Ripped In Pieces!

A TIDY POEM

Right then! It's time to tidy up the sky!
That's enough of your cheek! Don't ask me why!
I have told you a thousand times today
To put every one of those clouds away!
I've said it once, and I'll say it again,
You're just not old enough to play with rain!
Hey! You heard me! Leave those mountains alone!
Put them down! Right away! I don't like your tone.

And I don't care if you're a God in Heaven,
No pudding for you and bed at seven!

SELLOUT

Sell the birds, discount trees,
Charge for every, single breeze.

Put a price upon the air.
Can't afford it? We don't care.

Don't protest, or scream or shout.
Profit's what it's all about.

Wood's a stock, and every share
Is money growing into air.

Dreamers, poets, walking through
Private forests. We will sue!

Let the leaves be chained with locks.
Go home, turn on your goggle box.

Forget the plight of every tree,
It's all about economy.

Leaves are Like Traffic Lights

SUPERFAST

I'm a turbo-charged tree,
Yeah! Birdies like to hang out with me.

I do nought to sixty (metres high)
In only three (hundred years).

Yeah! I'm a turbo-charged tree.
With a cool wind behind me

I really start movin'
And my leaves are groovin'.

Yeah! I'm the turbo-charged tree.
Check out my canopy,

'Cos I'm the turbo-charged tree.
Air conditioning's free

And you know it's so cool
How I'm powered by hybrid fuel.

The way that it's done
Is by soaking up sun,

Plus, my roots love a drink.
Now I know what you think,

Leaves are Like Traffic Lights

That I'm a turbo-charged tree
Savin' the planet for free.

No emissions, nothin' to hide
I even get rid of your carbon-dioxide.

Listen up, I'm on your side,
Don't chop me down, commit suicide!

Cos I'm a turbo-charged tree,
Admit it man, you need me,
Otherwise — you're history!

ANDREW FUSEK PETERS

THE WHOLE WIDE WOOD

Let's go!
To the wood, where trees are masted ships
and we can sail a river of leaves.

Let's go!
Our den needs mending. We'll make it snug for winter,
gather brush and branches,
pick dry grass to weave it all together.
Then, like happy dogs, we'll loll inside
and say how warm we are in this fine place.

Let's go!
There are leaves to scoop and scuff and paddle through,
dry, tumbling currents that lap at our ankles.
We're leaf waders! Making our way to adventure.

Let's go!
We must find sticks — of perfect length and shape.
Explorers must have sticks:
to hold up high,
for most important poking of holes,
stirring of muddy puddles
and shaking,
fiercely.
Let's go!
We'll slip, like shadows, from trunk to trunk,

and spy on beetles and rabbits.
We'll keep careful lookout, keep check
that the curtains of dark in the heart of the woods
stay closed.

Let's go!
Where trees are turrets, castles, thrones,
where the squat, hollow oak
can be worn like a cloak
when we step inside
its rasping, bark folds.

Let's go!

ANDREW FUSEK PETERS

CHANT

Lemon, Larch, Laburnum, Lime,
This is the way we work our rhyme.

Chestnut Sweet and Flowering Cherry,
Today I'm mad, tomorrow merry.

Orange, Olive, Old Man Oak,
Give us a kiss and tell us a joke.

Pomegranate, Prickly Pear,
Does he love me, do I dare?

Beech, Bay, Blackthorn, Box,
Cut off all your curly locks.

Almond, Apple, Ash and Alder,
Will I be famous when I'm older?

Wych Elm, Walnut, Weeping Willow,
Lay your head on sleepy pillow.

Honeysuckle, Hazel, Hornbeam,
Hop to the dance and hope to dream.

Lemon, Larch, Laburnum, Lime,
This is the way we work our rhyme.

ANSWERS TO RIDDLES

A Fussy Riddle (page 37) Broom
Riddle Me Read (page 45) Book
Loop The Loop (page 70) Swallow
Riddle Me Time (page 75) Year/months/weeks/days
A Very Thin Riddle (page 84) Paper